IT'S TIME TO EAT SOURSOPS

It's Time to Eat SOURSOPS

Walter the Educator

Silent King Books
A WhichHead Entertainment Imprint

Copyright © 2025 by Walter the Educator

All rights reserved. No part of this book may be reproduced in any manner whatsoever without written per- mission except in the case of brief quotations embodied in critical articles and reviews.

First Printing, 2024

Disclaimer

This book is a literary work; the story is not about specific persons, locations, situations, and/or circumstances unless mentioned in a historical context. Any resemblance to real persons, locations, situations, and/or circumstances is coincidental. This book is for entertainment and informational purposes only. The author and publisher offer this information without warranties expressed or implied. No matter the grounds, neither the author nor the publisher will be accountable for any losses, injuries, or other damages caused by the reader's use of this book. The use of this book acknowledges an understanding and acceptance of this disclaimer.

It's Time to Eat SOURSOPS is a collectible early learning book by Walter the Educator suitable for all ages belonging to Walter the Educator's Time to Eat Book Series. Collect more books at WaltertheEducator.com

USE THE EXTRA SPACE TO TAKE NOTES AND DOCUMENT YOUR MEMORIES

SOURSOPS

It's time to eat, come take a look,

It's Time to Eat
Soursops

A fruit as fun as a storybook.

The soursop's here, both sweet and tart,

A tasty treat to fill your heart!

Its skin is green, with spiky scales,

It hides a treasure that never fails.

Inside it's soft, so white and sweet,

A tropical fruit that's hard to beat!

Cut it open, take it slow,

The creamy pulp will start to show.

But watch for seeds, they're shiny and black,

Pick them out, then have your snack!

Soursop tastes like candy dreams,

With hints of pineapple, mango, and creams.

It's tangy and sweet, a magical mix,

A flavor that gives your tongue a fix!

It's Time to Eat
Soursops

From warm lands with lots of sun,

Soursop trees grow, their work is done.

They give us fruit, their special gift,

To share and eat, it gives us a lift!

Some like it fresh, in juicy bites,

Others in smoothies, creamy delights.

No matter how, it's fun to eat,

The soursop fruit is a yummy treat!

Its smell is sweet, a tropical breeze,

Like sunshine swaying through the trees.

A sniff, a taste, it's pure delight,

A soursop snack makes everything right.

Look at its shape, so bumpy and round,

A fruit like this is fun to be found.

Every bite feels cool and bright,

It's Time to Eat
Soursops

It's nature's gift, both day and night!

Thank you, soursop, for all you do,

You're healthy, tasty, and good for us too!

A fruit that makes us smile so wide,

You're full of joy, a treat worldwide.

So gather close, let's share and cheer,

Soursop time is finally here!

With every bite, let's laugh and sing,

It's Time to Eat
Soursops

The soursop fruit is the snack we bring!

ABOUT THE CREATOR

Walter the Educator is one of the pseudonyms for Walter Anderson. Formally educated in Chemistry, Business, and Education, he is an educator, an author, a diverse entrepreneur, and he is the son of a disabled war veteran. "Walter the Educator" shares his time between educating and creating. He holds interests and owns several creative projects that entertain, enlighten, enhance, and educate, hoping to inspire and motivate you. Follow, find new works, and stay up to date with Walter the Educator™

at WaltertheEducator.com

www.ingramcontent.com/pod-product-compliance
Lightning Source LLC
LaVergne TN
LVHW052015060526
838201LV00059B/4040